Citing Cyberspace

to accompany

Lester

Writing Research Papers: A Complete Guide

Eighth Edition

James D. Lester
Austin Peay State University

LONGMAN

An imprint of Addison Wesley Longman, Inc.

New York • Reading, Massachusetts • Menlo Park, California • Harlow, England
Don Mills, Ontario • Sydney • Mexico City • Madrid • Amsterdam

Citing Cyberspace t/a Writing Research Papers: A Complete Guide, Eighth Edition, by James D. Lester

ISBN: 0-321-02145-2

2 3 4 5 6 7 8 9 10 - CB - 00 99 98 97

Contents

1

Finding Resources on the Internet

The **Internet,** a worldwide computer network, offers instant access to hundreds, even thousands, of computer files relating to almost any subject, including articles, illustrations, sound and video clips, and raw data. For easy access to this network, most researchers now use the **Word Wide Web,** which is a set of files connected by hypertext links and accessed by means of a **browser,** such as *Netscape Navigator* and *Microsoft Explorer.*

Sets of computer instructions called HTTP (*hypertext transfer protocol)* and HTML (*hypertext markup language*) make it simple to connect files (or *sites*) to each other using *hypertext links*. Links are "hot" text or icons that, when clicked, instruct the computer to perform certain functions, such as to go to another file. You will know that text is "hot" when it is underlined and colored blue; also, with most browsers the pointer changes form when it moves over "hot" text.

Web browsers are able to find files because each file on the Web is given a unique address that follows a specific format. An address in this format is called a Uniform Resource Locator (URL). Thus, by clicking the computer mouse on various URL addresses or icons, you can find specific articles within this vast network (web). Let's look at one URL. It follows this pattern: protocol/server.domain/directory/file.

http://www.georgetown.edu/labyrinth/library/library_catalogues.html

The *protocol* is a technological process for transmitting data. The protocol gives instructions that tell the computer how to handle incoming data. Without the protocol and without an address, your files cannot move on the Internet. Other Internet protocols that you will see are FTP, Gopher, Telnet, and more, which are explained below.

The *server,* in this case *georgetown,* is the computer upon which this file has been saved.

The *domain* names the organization that is feeding information into the server with a *suffix* to label the type of organization—*.com* commercial; *.edu* educational; *.gov* government; *.mil* military; *.net* network organization; and *.org* nonprofit organization. Often, knowing just the protocol and the server.domain name will get you to a home site from which you can search deeper for files. The site *www.georgetown.edu* will take you to Georgetown University's home page, where you can ask for a specific directory, such as *labyrinth,* which offers the researcher a wide assortment of files. In this case, the directory *library* contains a file called *library_catalogues,* which is a catalogue of libraries and ways to access them.

The closing code, *html,* signals to readers that *hypertext markup language* was used to write the files.

Using a Search Engine

Search engines are Internet sites that look for and index other sites. Many search engines provide both subject directories and key-word searches. General, commercial sites provide access to subject menus and key-word searches. The commercial sites will entice you with advertisements for various products, but they do an excellent job of directing you to a wide variety of sources. These are a few of the most popular:

AltaVista	http://altavista.digital.com/
Excite	http://www.excite.com
Hotbot	http://www.hotbot.com
Infoseek	http://guide.infoseek.com
Lycos	http://www.lycos.com
Open Text Index	http://www.opentext.com/omw/
	f-omw.html
Search	http://www.search.com
Webcrawler	http://webcrawler.com
Yahoo	http://www.yahoo.com

New search engines appear almost monthly, many specializing in one area, such as *WWWomen* (women's studies), *TribalVoice* (Native American Studies), *Bizweb* (business studies). In addition, large Web sites sometimes have search engines just for themselves.

Educational search engines provide subject indexes to the various disciplines (Humanities or Sciences) and to subtopics under those headings (History, Literature, Biochemistry, etc.). These four will help you get started:

Clearinghouse	http://www.clearinghouse.net
Internet Public Library	http://ipl.sils.umich.edu/
Planet Earth	http://www.nosc.mil/
	planet_earth/info.html
Virtual Library SavvySearch	http:/www.cs.colostate.edu/
	~dreiling/smartform.html

Bookmarks

Most Web programs, such as Netscape, include a bookmarks tool that enables you to save addresses for quick access. When you find a search engine or a file that you need to access on a regular basis, make a bookmark to the site so that you can revisit it with just a click of the mouse. For example, in Netscape simply click on *Bookmarks*, then click on *Add Bookmark*. This will automatically add the URL to the list of bookmarks. In Microsoft Internet Explorer use the button bar marked *Favorites* to make your bookmarks. Note: if you are working at a university computer laboratory, do not add bookmarks to the hard drive. Instead, save the bookmarks to your disk by using *save as* in the *file* menu of Netscape.

Using a Subject Directory

A **subject directory** will take you through a sequence of Internet subjects. Subject-tree directories are hierarchical; that is, they move you methodically to more narrow topics. You might start with *history*, move to *military history*, move to *Civil War History*, move to *Civil War Battles*, and arrive finally at *The Battle at Gettysburg*. In effect, the subject directory will have carried you from the general to the specific. Use this technique when you have no preconceived notion about the topic you wish to write about.

Using a key-word search

When you know your topic, perform a key-word search using the words you would like to find in the title, description, or text of an Internet site. For example, to find information on Robert E. Lee's role at the Battle of Gettysburg, you would enter the words:

Gettysburg and battle and Robert E. Lee

which will present a list of such sites as:

http://gettysburg.welcome.com/battle.html
or
http://www.gettybg.com/battle.html

You can then skim the articles on the monitor to determine their relevance to your research efforts.

Tips for Searching

1. If you search for a common or general word, such as *gettysburg*, you will get a mammoth search of every document that contains this term. Use lower case words, if you like, because they will also find capitalized words (e.g. "gettysburg" will find *gettysburg, Gettysburg, GETTYSBURG*).

NOTE: Not all search engines use words and symbols interchangeably, so you may need to read the HELP menu of each one for details.

2. If you provide two or more words with *and* or the "+" sign between each one, the search engine will find only sources that combine all words.

gettysburg *and* Lee
gettysburg + Lee

3. Attach a *not* or a minus (-) sign in front of words that *must not* be a part of the search:

gettysburg + Lee - Lincoln
gettysburg *and* Lee *not* Lincoln

This request will give you documents that mention gettysburg and Robert E. Lee but will eliminate any documents that include Lincoln's name.

4. Use a *t:* to restrict the search to sites that contain the title, be it a book, article, poem, document, or speech:

t: "gettysburg address"

5. Use quotation marks around two words to make them one unit (although proper names do not need quotation marks).

"stone henge" + Thomas Hardy

This request will give you documents that combine both Stone Henge and Thomas Hardy. The use of phrases is perhaps the best way to limit the number of hits by the search engine. Compare:

gettysburg and lincoln and address (40,000 documents found)

"Lincoln's Gettysburg Address" (200 documents found)

Therefore, make your request in phrases whenever possible; that is, ask for "migraine headaches" (2,000 hits), not "migraine and headaches" (10,000 hits). Netscape Navigator Gold 3, for example, gives you a search option for *phrase* as well as by *any* word or *all* words.

What should you do, however, when the search engine only produces one or two sources or useless sources? First, you can try another search engine because not all search engines work in the same way, so they give different results. Second, you can change the key-word selection.

Evaluating Internet Sources

The Internet supplies mammoth amounts of material, some of it excellent and some not so good. You must make judgments about the validity and veracity of these materials. In addition to your common sense judgment, here are a few guidelines:

1. Use the "edu" and "org" sites. Usually, these will be domains developed by an educational instutition, such as Ohio State University, or by a professional organization, such as the American Psychological Association. The "gov" (government) and "mil" (military) sites usually have realiable materials. The "com" (commercial) sites become suspect for several reasons: (1) they are selling advertising space, (2) they often charge you for access to their files, (3) they can be ISP sites (Internet Service Provider) which people pay to use and to post their "material." Although some ISP sites might have good information, they are usually no more reliable than vanity presses or want ads.

2. Look for the *professional* affiliation of the writer, which you will find in the opening credits or in an Email address.

3. Look for a bibliography that accompanies the article, which will indicate the scholarly nature of this writer's work.

4. Usenet discussion groups offer valuable information at times, but some articles lack sound, fundamental reasoning or evidence to support the opinions.

5. Treat Email messages as "mail," not scholarly articles.

6. Does the site give you hypertext links to other professional sites or to commercial sites? Links to other educational sites serve as a modern bibliography to more reliable sources. Links to commercial sites are often attempts to sell you something.

Accessing Online Magazines and Journals

Search out articles on your topic by accessing online journals, magazines and newspapers.

Journals. Begin by looking for scholarly journals that might be online. First, try making a key-word query if you know the title, such as *Psycholoquy,* a social science journal.

Second, if you want a comprehensive list of periodicals on a subject, access a search engine where you might find them in a subject directory. In *Yahoo,* for example, this writer selected Social Science from the key directory, clicked on Journals, then on Social Work, and accessed links to five online journals.

Third, access a search engine and use a key-word search using the words *journals* or *periodicals* and the name of your discipline. For example, this writer accessed *Alta Vista* and used a key-word search for "journals + social work." From the list provided, one of the sites, *Social*

Work and the Internet-Journals, produced links to 23 on-line journals devoted to social work. In another search, a request for "women's studies + journals" produced a list of journals, such as *Feminist Collections, Resources for Feminist Research,* or *Differences.* By accessing one of these links, you can examine abstracts and articles.

Many of the online periodicals offer an index to articles and some even provide key-word searches. Of more importance, these journal sites will often provide full-text articles from hard-to-find periodicals that may not be housed in your library. (Caution: some journals will require a fee or require you to join the association before permitting access.)

Magazines. Several directories exist for searching out magazine articles:

Ecola's 24-Hour Newstand	http://www.ecola.com/new/
Electric Library	http://www3.elibrary.com/
Pathfinder	http://pathfinder.com/
Monster Magazine List	http://enews.com/monster/ index.html
Ziff-Davis Magazines	http://www.zdnet.com/hom/ filters/mags.html

The *Electric Library,* for example, offers key-word searches as well as a directory. This writer used "child abuse" for a key-word search, and the engine found 30 articles on this topic in such periodicals as *Futurist, Mother Jones,* and *Research on Social Work Practice.*

Newspapers. Most major magazines maintain commercial sites. Here are a few:

The Chronicle of Higher Education	http://www.chronicle.com
The New York Times	http://www.nytimes.com
USA Today	http://www.usatoday.com
U.S. News Online	http://www.usnews.com
Wall Street Journal	http://www.wsj.com

Using Online Versions Rather than Print Versions

There are certain advantages to the use of the online versions of these works. First, you can find them almost instantly on the monitor screen rather than having to search microfilm or microfiche. Second, you can use the online indexes or search engines to find an appropriate article on your topic. Third, you can save or print out an abstract or article without the hassle of using the photocopying machine. Fourth, you can download material to your disk and, where appropriate, insert it into your research paper. However, disadvantages also exist. You may have to subscribe at a modest cost. The texts may not be the same as printed versions; some may be digest versions of the original. Abstracts may not accurately represent the full article. Therefore, act with caution.

Using Gopher, FTP, Telnet, and Other Protocols

Although HTTP sources now dominate the Web, valuable material still exists on other protocols, such as **Gopher, FTP,** and **Telnet.** These sources will look different because they have no hypertext format (they are not linked to other sources) and most do not have graphics and color. *Gopher* is an Internet browser that burrows deeper and deeper into layers of information, unlike the Web, which allows you to move from site to site regardless of level of specificity.

Gopher requires you to select items from a general menu, then from a more specific menu, and so on, until you arrive at a specific site. Its name comes from the Golden Gophers at the University of Minnesota, where the software was developed. Unlike *http* sites, Gopher will not transfer you quickly from site to site. If you see a plain text file with no hot keys, it is probably a Gopher site. They look like this Gopher menu from the University of Virginia library:

psyc.95.6.01.group-selection.1.caporael
psyc.95.6.02.language-network.11miikkulainen
psyc.95.6.03.language-network.12.miikkulainen
psyc.95.6.04.language-network.13.miikkulainnen
psyc.95.6.05.sex-brain.1.fitch
psyc.95.6.06.memory-brain.1.klimesch

Fortunately, most Gopher files have been redesigned as files for the World Wide Web. Note: the process for accessing Gopher files varies from place to place, so you will need specific instructions at your school. Two keyword search engines for Gopher are:

gopher://veronica.psi.net:2347/7-tl

gopher://empire.nysernet.org:2347/7

File Transfer Protocol (FTP) is a step-by-step process by which you copy computer files—text, graphics, video, sound, and so forth—from the Internet into your computer file. Thus, you can access files then use FTP to copy what you need. As with Gopher, you will need specific instructions for the system at your school. In some cases you will need a user account.

Telnet, which will give you access to various computer databases, will require the use of directories and menus to find items. Unlike FTP, it is not a protocol for file transfer but a remote operations protocol. Telnet is a protocol that lets you access a computer somewhere on the net and use it as though it were your own terminal. To do this, you will need a username or password that will permit you to log in and begin working. In Netscape you can access a known program by selecting *Options* ➔ *General Preferences* ➔ *Apps.* At the window you can install the Telnet client that will work within Netscape. Again, you will need to get help for your specific system from a librarian, instructor, or an expert at the computer center.

Listserv provides ongoing Email discussion on technical and educational topics. To participate, you must have an Email address and, in some cases, subscribe to the list. To access a Listserv, write to a server, such as <listserv@listserv.net> for a list of discussion groups on your topic. For example, student Wes Cochran made this request for groups on "health":

To:	listserv@listserv.net
Subject:	info
Message:	List Global Health

The return Email message gave the student a list of discussion groups from which to choose. The student sent this message:

To:	listserv@listserv.net
Subject:	subscribe
Message	subscribe SHS SHS@UTKVM1 (Student Health Services)

He soon received word that his subscription had been activated, along with instructions for participating and the means of cancelling the subscription once his research had ended.

Another way to find discussion groups is through a key-word search for "List of LISTSERV lists" at one of the search engines (see page 4). Remember, you must subscribe in order to join the group; subscriptions are free in most cases.

A few additional aspects of Listserv are FAQ, lurking, and moderated and unmoderated lists. FAQ (frequently asked questions) documents provide answers to the questions that new members of the group are likely to ask.

Usenet provides access to newsgroups (discussion groups). Unlike Listserv messages that arrive via Email, you can access Usenet discussion groups on the Internet. One list of newgroup lists can be found at this site:

http://www.dejanews.com

Some Internet search engines, such as *Alta Vista,* give you the choice of searching Usenet rather than the Web. Also, some versions of browsers, such as Netscape, can be set to read newsgroups and perform key-word searches of them.

This text, however, does not pretend to be a manual on all possible sites and protocols, and the sites change almost weekly. However, you should realize that many search engines exist for your particular needs. Seek authoritative advice on using the wide variety of documents.

Using CD-ROM

You will find *CD-ROM* in two forms. One version is a disk that you load into your computer. Many games come in this form, but scholarly material is also available. The other is a disk or set of disks preloaded as a database into the computer(s) at your library. For general information as you begin your research, consult encyclopedias on the individual disks, such as *Grolier's Encyclopedia, Encarta,* or *Electronic Classical Library.* Like the Internet, a CD-ROM disk now makes it possible to read text (such as a play by Shakespeare), download selected passages, and paste them quickly into your text. With disks loaded onto your CD-ROM drive, such as *The History of American Literature* or *America's Civil War: A Nation Divided,* you can examine the biographical and critical articles and, again, download material to your paper (while giving scholarly credit, of course). Finally, many large and hefty research tools, such as the *Oxford English Dictionary* or the *McGraw-Hill Enclopedia of World Economies*, have been published in convenient CD-ROM. Libraries may not hold all CD-ROMs relevant to your research. Look for additional disks in other locations at your school: department offices, department libraries, and individual professors' offices.

UMI-ProQuest, Silverplatter, InfoTrac, and *Eric* are CD-ROM databases loaded into your library's computer, Like the search engines on the Internet, these databases direct you to articles on your listed subject. For full discussion, see *Writing Research Papers: A Complete Guide*, pages 37-38.

Examining Library Holdings Via Internet Access

Consult **libraries** through the Internet. Many libraries now offer an OPAC (Online Public Access Catalog), which will allow you to search their collections for books, videos, dissertations, audio tapes, special collections, and other items. You may sometimes order books through interlibrary loan online. Additionally, some of the libraries now post full-text documents, downloadable bibliographies, databases, and links to other sites. Therefore, if you need identification of all books on a topic, as copyrighted and housed in Washington, DC, consult:

Library of Congress http://www.loc.gov

This site allows you to search by word, phrase, name, title, series, and number. It also provides special features, such as an American Memory Home Page, full-text legislative information, and exhibitions. You can view, for example, the various drafts of Lincoln's *Gettysburg Address*.

For an Internet overview of libraries, their holdings, and addresses, consult:

LIBCAT   http://www.metronet.lib.mn.us/lc/lc1.html
LIBWEB   http://sunsite.berkeley.edu/libweb

For many library connections, the library's computer will prompt you with a public-access login name, so follow the directions for entering and exiting the programs.

2

Finding Internet Sources for
A Selected Discipline

The following list cannot be up-to-date nor all-inclusive simply because the Web is growing like an adolescent youngster. Nevertheless, these sites, in addition to the ones found by your key-word and subject searches, will launch your investigation of Internet resources. We have listed those disciplines most used by freshman for their research. Keep in mind that a key-word search will find one of these sites even if the Universal Resource Locator (URL) has changed.

Truncating the Address

If you have problems accessing a particular site, try truncating the address; that is, cut items from the end. For example, if you have trouble accessing this address:

http://www.emory.edu/WHSC/medweb.medlibs.html

try cutting it to:

http://www.emory.edu

then, within this main page of the Web site, you can go in search of the medical files.

Art

The Parthnet

http://home.mtholyoke.edu/~klconner/parthnet.html

This resource gives you information on ancient and classical art, the treasures of the Renaissance, 19th Century American works, impressionism, and many other periods. It will also link you with major museums and their collections.

World Wide Arts Resources

    http://wwar.world-arts-resources.com

    This site provides an artist index as well as an index to exhibits, festivals, meetings, and performances. Its search engine will take you to fine arts departments, online courses, syllabi, and art institutions.

WebLouvre

    http://sunsite.unc.edu/wm/

    This internet version of the Musee du Louvre enables you to visit the painting exhibits, the sculptures, the Louvre's Auditorium, and miscellaneous exhibits, such as the medieval art collection. It even includes a short tour of Paris.

Astronomy

American Astronomical Society

    http://www.aas.org

    This site gives you the *Astrophysical Journal*, providing articles, reviews, and educational information. It gives links to other astronomical sites on the Web.

Mount Wilson Observatory

    http://www.mtwilson.edu

    This site takes you into the Mount Wilson Observatory for outstanding photography of the universe and for online journals, documents, agencies, and activities in astronomical science.

The Northern Lights Planetarium, Norway

    http://www.uit.no/npt/homepage-npt.en.html

    This site takes you into the planetarium, displays the northern lights in vivid colors, and enables you to research such topics as *Aurora Borealis.*

The Universe at Our Doorstep

http://neptune.cgy.oanet.comp

This site links you to NASA programs, such as the space station, the shuttle program, or Project Galileo. It provides maps of the planets, views of Earth from many different angles, and plenty of planetary information.

Athletics

Outside Online

http://outside.starwave.com:80

This Web site is devoted to outdoor sports, such as biking, skiing, backpacking, and camping, with reviews of current sports and equipment.

Sportsline USA

http://www.sportsline.com/index.html

This site focuses on professional sports, such as auto racing, baseball, golf, and many others. Its Newsroom page provides news, photographs, and links to other sites.

ESPNET Sports Zone

http://espnet.sportzone.com

This site, provided by the ESPN sports network, gives up-to-date sports information as well as behind-the-scene articles.

Business

All Business Network

http://www.all-biz.com

This site provides a search engine to businesses with relevant information for the following: newsletters, organizations, news groups, and magazines.

Finance: The World Wide Web Virtual Library

http://www.cob.ohio-state.edu/dept/fin/overview.html

The Finance Department of Ohio State University has established a site that will link you to hundreds of articles and resource materials on banks, insurers, market news, jobs, and miscellaneous data for students.

Nijenrode Business Webserver

http://www.nigenrode.nl/nbr/index.html

This site serves primarily students and faculty at business schools with a search engine that finds news, business journals, career opportunities in accounting, banking, finance, marketing, and other related fields.

Communication

Communication Resources on the Web

http://alnilam.ucs.indiana.edu:1027/sources/comm.html

This large database takes you to resources and Web sites on associations, book reviews, bibliographies, libraries, media, information science programs, and departments of communication in various universities.

Computer and Internet Technology

Byte Magazine

> http://www.byte.comp

> This site provides the major print articles from *Byte* magazine with product information on computer products, such as Netscape or Wordperfect.

Internet Society

> http://www.isoc.org/indextxt.html

> This site is supported by the companies, agencies, and foundations that launched the Internet and that keep it functioning. It gives you vital information with articles from the ISOC Forum newsletter.

OCP's Guide to Online High Tech Resources

> http://ocprometheus.org

> With a search engine that performs key-word searches, this site brings you a wealth of full-text articles, online magazines, technical documents, and Web links to high-tech issues.

Virtual Computer Library

> http://www.utexas.edu/computer/ucl

> This site gives you access to academic computing centers at the major universities along with books, articles, and bibliographies.

Current Events

New York Times on the Web

> http://www.nytimes.com

> This sites presents current news of the day from the print edition with

compilations of articles on Arts and Leisure, Travel, and other special features.

Trib.com--The Internet Newspaper

http://www.trib.com

This site is an online newspaper with complete articles on news, weather, and sports from around the world with links to Reuter's, the Associated Press, and other wire services.

USA Today

http://www.usatoday.com

USA Today online contains sections on news, life, money, sports, and special features. An index gives access to previous articles and a search engine takes you to specific articles on your chosen subject.

Wall Street Journal

http://www.wsj.com

This online edition features headlines and some articles from the print edition with a classroom edition for secondary school students and teachers.

Education

Chronicle of Education

http://chronicle.merit.edu

This site gives you "Academe This Week" from *The Chronicle of Education*, a weekly printed magazine about education on the undergraduate and graduate levels. You will need to be a subscriber to gain full access.

Educom

> http://educom.edu
>
> This site has full-text online articles with a focus on educational technology in its *Educom Review*, a focus on information technology in *Edupage*, and general news from *Educom Update*.

Edweb

> http://edweb.cnidr.org:90
>
> This site focuses on educational issues and resource materials for grades K-12 with articles on Web education, Web history, and Web resources.

Online Educational Resources

> http://quest.arc.nasa.gov/OER
>
> This site by NASA provides an extensive list of educational articles and documents on everything from the space shuttle to planetary exploration.

ERIC (Educational Resource and Information Center)

> http://ericir.syr.edu/ithome
>
> ERIC is considered the primary source of research information for most educators. It contains about one million documents, available by a key-word search, on all aspects of teaching and learning, lesson plans, administration, bibliographies, and almost any topic related to the classroom.

Environment

Envirolink
http://envirolink.org

> This site has a search engine that allows access to environmental

articles, photographs, action alerts, organizations, and additional Web sources.

Medicine and Global Survival

http://www.healthnet.org/MGS/MGS.html

This online journal features articles on environmental destruction, overpopulation, infectious diseases, the consequences of war, and, in general, the health of the globe. It provides links to other journals, newsletters, and government documents that explore environmental issues.

Government

Bureau of the Census

http://www.census.gov

This site from the U. S. Department of Commerce provides census data on geography, housing, and the population. It allows you to examine specific information about your targeted county.

Fedworld

http:///www.fedworld.gov

This site gives you links to Web sites of the government departments as well as lists of free catalogs. It links you to the Internal Revenue Service and other government agencies.

Library of Congress

http://www.lcweb.loc.gov

This site provides the Library of Congress catalog online for books by author, subject, and title. It also links you to historical collections and research tools.

Thomas

http://thomas.loc.gov

This site gives you access to congressional legislation and documents indexed by topic, by bill number if you have it, and by title. It also allows you to search the Congressional Record, The Constitution, and other government documents. It links you to the House, the Senate, the Government Printing Office, and the General Accounting Office.

White House Web

http://www.whitehouse.gov

This site provides a graphical tour, messages from the President and the Vice-President, and accounts of life at the White House. Visitors to this site can even leave a message for the president in the guest book.

Health and Medicine

Global Health Network

http://www.pitt.edu/HOME/GHNet.html

This site provides you with access to documents in public health as provided by scholars at The World Health Organization, NASA, The Pan American Health Organization, and others. It links you to agencies, organizations, and health networks.

Martindale's Health Science Guide

http://www-sci.lib.uci.edu/HSG/HSGuide.html

This giant database gives you access to several medical centers for online journals and documents in medicine, nursing, nutrition, public health, medical law, and veterinary work.

Medweb: Medical Libraries

http://www.emory.edu/WHSC/medweb.medlibs.html

Emory University provides a site that connects you with medical libraries and their storehouses of information. It also gives links to other health-related Web sites.

National Institutes of Health

http://www.nih.gov

NIH leads the nation in medical research, so this site provides substantive information on numerous topics, from cancer and diabetes to malpractice and medical ethics. It provides links to online journals for the most recent news in medical science.

History

Archiving Early America

http://earlyamerica.com

This site displays 18th Century documents in their original form for reading and downloading, such as the Bill of Rights and the speeches of Washington, Paine, Jefferson, and others.

Humanities Hub

http://www.gu.edu.au/gwis/hub.hom.html

This site provides resources in the humanities and social sciences with links to anthropology, architecture, cultural studies, film, gender studies, government, history, philosophy, sociology, and women.

The Humbul Gateway

http://info.ox.ac.uk/departments/humanities/international.html

This site provides historical resources, references, libraries, and bulletin boards with links to downloadable texts.

Literature

The English Server

> http://english-server.hss.cmu.edu

> Carnegie Mellon University provides academic resources in the humanities, including drama, fiction, film, television, and history, with the added bonus of calls for papers and a link for downloading freeware and shareware.

Literature Directory

> http://web.syr.edu/~fjzwick/sites/lit.html

> As the name describes it, this site provides a directory with links to specific pieces of literature.

Project Gutenberg

> http://promo.net/pg

> This site provides literary texts in the public domain that can be downloaded via FTP and that are divided into three divisions: light literature such as fables, heavy literature such as *The Scarlet Letter*, and reference works.

Voice of the Shuttle

> http://humanitas.ucsb.edu

> For the literary scholar, this site gives a massive collection of bibliographies, textual criticism, newsgroups, and links to classical studies, history, philosophy, and other related disciplines.

Philosophy

The American Philosophical Association

http://www.oxy.edu/apa.html

This site provides articles, bibliographies, software, a bulletin board, Gopher server, and links to other philosophical sites containing college courses, journals, texts, and newsletters.

Psychology

Clinical Psychology Resources

http://www.psychologic.uni-bonn.de/kap/links_20.htm

This site features articles on assessment, behavior, disorders, psychotherapy, and other related issues. It has links to online journals and psychology organizations. It provides a key-word index to both articles and books.

Psych Web

http://www.gasou.edu/psychweb/psychweb.htm#top

This site features a collection of articles from *Psychiatric Times*, reports from the National Institute of Health, information from universities, and links to psychology journals and other sites on the Internet. It includes, online, Freud's *The Interpretation of Dreams*.

Religion

Comparative Religion

http://weber.u.washington.edu/~madin

This comprehensive site gives references and resources to all religions and religious studies and religious organizations.

Vanderbilt Divinity School

http://www.library.vanderbilt.edu/divinity/homelib.html

This source gives you references and interpretations to the Bible, links to other religious Web sites, and on-line journals, such as *Biblical Archaeologist.*

Science

The Academy of Natural Sciences Related Links

http://www.acnatsci.org/links.html

This site will link you to hundreds of articles and resource materials on various issues and topics in the natural sciences.

Discovery Channel Online

http://www.discovery.com

This site is an online version of television's Discovery Channel, and it features a key-word search engine.

Discover Magazine

http://www.dc.enews.com/magazines/discover

This site is a online version of *Discover Magazine*, including the texts of many articles. Its Archive Library enables you to examine articles from past issues.

National Academy of Sciences

http://www.nas.edu

This comprehensive site combines the resources of the National Academy of Engineering, the Institute of Medicine, and the National Research Council. It focuses on math and science education, and it has links to scientific societies.

Network Science

http://www.awod.com/netsci

The NetSci engine searches out biotechnological literature with links to other scientific Web sites. It focuses mainly on chemistry and pharmaceuticals.

Social Science

Political Science Resources on the Web

http://www.lib.umich.edu/libhome/Documents.center/polisci.html

This site at the University of Michigan is a vast data file on government information--local, state, federal, foreign, and international. It is a good site for political theory and international relations with links to dissertations, periodicals, reference sources, university courses, and other social science information.

Praxis

http://caster.ssu.upenn.edu/~restes/praxis.html

This site provides a massive collection of articles on socioeconomic topics with links to other social science resources.

Social Science Information Gateway (SOSIG)

http://sosig.esrc.bris.ac.uk/Welcome.html#socialsciences

The SOSIG site provides a key-word search that makes available to you many Web sites in an alphabetical list.

Sociology

http://hakatai.mcli.dist.maricopa.edu/smc/ml/sociology.html

This site gives you access to hundreds of sites that provide articles and resource materials on almost all aspects of sociology issues.

Women's Studies

The Women's Resource Project

http://sunsite.unc.edu/cheryb/women

This site links you to libraries on the Web that have collections on Women's Studies. It also has links to women's programs and women's resources on the Web.

Women's Studies Resources

http:www.inform.umd.edu:8080/EdRes/Topic/WomensStudies

This site features a search engine for a key-word search to women's issues and provides directories to bibliographies, classic texts, references, course syllabi from various universities, and links to other Web sites.

Women's Studies Librarian

http://www.library.wisc.edu/libraries/WomensStudies

This site at the University of Wisconsin provides information on important contributions by women in Science, Health, and Technology with links to their activities in literature, government, and business.

Writing

Research Links for Writers

http://www.siu.edu/departments/cola/english/seraph9k/research.html

This site gives you a method for finding and accessing various articles and discussions about writing, especially research writing.

Citing Cyberspace

WWW Resources for Rhetoric and Composition

    http.//www.ind.net/Internet/comp.html

    This site provides a number of links to issues on writing and the teaching of writing.

Internet Resources for English Teachers and Students

    http://www.umass.edu/english/resource.html

    This site at the University of Massachusetts provides links to articles and instructional materials for the English class.

3

Citing Electronic Sources in MLA Style

The standards for documenting sources in papers in the humanities, foreign languages, and various other fields is established by the Modern Language Association, as published in the *MLA Handbook for Writers of Research Papers,* 4th edition, 1995. However, the MLA guidelines for online sources are still being formulated. As this guide goes to press, the MLA committee on documentation style plans to update the standards but has not finalized the format. Correspondence with the committee indicates that it wants researchers to cite the electronic source just as they would for a printed source and to add (1) the date of access and (2) the URL within angle brackets. In addition, the committee has begun formulating rules for the in-text citations to electronic sources. The suggestions here maintain the format of MLA citations for Web sites, newsgroups, Listserv, Gopher, and other protocols.

MLA Style for In-Text Citations

Currently, most Internet sources have no prescribed page numbers or numbered paragraphs. You cannot list a screen number because monitors differ. You cannot list the page numbers of a downloaded document because computer printers differ. Therefore, in most cases do not list a page number or a paragraph number. Here are the basic rules.

1. **Omit a page or paragraph number.** The marvelous feature of electronic text is that it is searchable, so your readers can find your quotation quickly with the FIND feature. Suppose that you have written the following:

One source advises against making the television industry the "scapegoat for violence" by advocating a focus on "deadlier and more significant causes:

```
inadequeate parenting, drugs, underclass rage,
unemployment and availability of weaponry" (UCLA
Television Violence Report 1996).
```

A reader who wants to investigate further will find your complete citation on your Works Cited page. There the reader will discover the Internet address for the article. After finding the article via a browser, (e.g., Netscape or Internet Explorer), the investigator can press EDIT, then FIND, and then type in a key phrase, such as *scapegoat for violence*. The software will immediately move the cursor to the passage shown above. That's much easier than counting through 46 paragraphs.

2. **Provide a paragraph number only if the source is prenumbered.** Some academic societies are urging scholars who write on the Internet to number their paragraphs, so if you find an article on the Internet that has numbered paragraphs, by all means supply that information in your citation.

```
The Insurance Institute for Highway Safety
emphasizes restraint first, saying, "Riding
unrestrained or improperly restrained in a motor
vehicle always has been the greatest hazard for
children" (par. 13).
```

```
The most common type of diabetes is non-insulin-
dependent-diabetes mellitus (NIDDM), which "affects
90% of those with diabetes and usually appears
after age 40" (Larson par. 3).
```

3. **Provide a page number only if numbers of the printed version are supplied.** In a few instances, you will find page numbers buried within brackets here and there throughout an article. These refer to the page numbers of the printed version of the document. In these cases, you should cite the page just as you would cite it for a printed source. Note this example:

De-nationalizing does not mean abolishing difference but abolishing the myth of identity that regulated and policed difference upholds. Thus, what is required is a reading of the frontiers and borders that are at /pp 17-18/ work within and against the pretensions to "greatness," to majority, of any national literature. That is to say, a finding of the minor and the evocation of its difference where it is not expected.

Readings argues that each literary culture should identify the minor literature as a part of its national identity, not just elevate its majority literature as its "greatness" (pp. 17-18).

World Wide Web Site

Robert B. Dove makes the distinction between a Congressional calendar day and a legislative day, noting, "A legislative day is the period of time following an adjournment of the Senate until another adjournment."

Commenting on Neolithic sites of the Southern Levant in the online magazine *Biblical Archaeologist*, E. B. Banning argues, the "Natufians set the stage for the development of large villages with an increasing reliance on cereal grains and legumes that could be cultivated." Banning's work shows that small villages often existed for a time only to disappear mysteriously, perhaps because of plagues, invaders, or--most likely--a nomadic way of life.

"Psychologically oriented techniques used to elicit confessions may undermine their validity" (Kassin, abstract).

Citing Cyberspace

E-Mail

One technical writing instructor, Jim Clemmer, bemoans the inability of hardware developers to maintain pace with the ingenuity of software developers (Email).

Listserv (Email Discussion Group)

Rosemary Camilleri has identified the book *Storyteller* for those interested in narrative bibliography.

HyperNews Posting

Abigail Ochberg reports on the use of algae in paper that "initially has a green tint to it, but unlike bleached paper, which turns yellow with age, this algae paper becomes whiter with age."

Gopher Site

In an essay in *Electronic Antiquity*, Richard Diamond explores the issue of blindness in *Oedipus Rex*:

> Thus Sophokles has us ask the question, who is blind? We must answer that Teiresias is physically blind, yet he sees himself and Oidipous' nature. Oidipous is physically sighted, but he is blind to himself, to his own nature.

Establishing the Credibility of the Source

In some instances, your instructors may expect you to indicate your best estimate of the scholarly value of a source. For example, the citation immediately below might read in this way in order to verify the validity of the source:

> The UCLA Center for Communication Policy, which conducted an intensive study of television violence during 1995, has advised against making the television industry the "scapegoat for violence" by advocating a focus on "deadlier and more significant causes: inadequate parenting, drugs, underclass rage, unemployment and availability of weaponry" (UCLA Television Violence Report 1996).

Here's another example:

> John Armstrong, a spokesperson for Public Electronic Access to Knowledge (PEAK), states:
>> As we venture into this age of biotechnology, many people predict gene manipulation will be a powerful tool for improving the quality of life. They foresee plants engineered to resist pests, animals designed to produce large quantities of rare medicinals, and humans treated by gene therapy to relieve suffering.

To learn more about the source of an Internet article, as in the case immediately above, learn to search out a home page. The address for Armstrong's article is <http://www.peak.org/~armstroj/america. html#Aims>, but by truncating the address to <http://www.peak.org/> you can learn about the organization that Armstrong represents.

If you are not certain about the credibility of a source, that is, it seemingly has no scholarly or educational basis, do not cite it or describe the source so that readers can make their own judgments:

> An Iowa non-profit organization, the Mothers for

Natural Law, says--but offers no proof--that eight major crops are affected by genetically engineered organisms--canola, corn, cotton, dairy products, potatoes, soybeans, tomatoes, and yellow crook-neck squash ('What's on the Market").

Online Magazine

Business Week reports that health-care inflation seems determined to climb because medical costs are increasing and could "hit double digits."

In *Kudzu*, Todd Brendan Fahey describes one of his characters in "Beach House" in this manner:
> Johnny was, by my estimation, a Casualty, though a functional one. He walked everywhere, and everywhere he walked, a bright, pleasant grin stretched his facial muscles, and he looked like a carpenter who had plied his trade well.

Government Document

The Web site *Thomas* provides the four-page outline to the *Superfund Cleanup Acceleration Act of 1997*, which will provoke community participation, enforce remedial actions, establish liability, and protect natural resources.

FTP (File Transfer Protocol) Sites

A. A. Kranidiotis shows in the following graph, downloaded from an FTP site, that, perceptually, "all the sounds corresponding to the points on the curve have the same intensity: this means that the ear has a large range where it is nearly linear (1000 to 8000 Hz), achieving better results on a little domain."

CD-ROM

Like Internet sources, the printout of an article from a CD-ROM source will differ from printer to printer; therefore do not cite page numbers unless original pagination is provided here and there within brackets.

Compton's Interactive Encyclopedia explains that the Abolition Society, which originated in England in 1787, appears to be the first organized group in opposition to slavery. Later, in 1823, the Anti-Slavery Society was formed by Thomas Fowell Buxton, who wielded power as a member of Parliament.

MLA Works Cited Entries

Include these items as appropriate to the source:

1. Author/editor name
2. Title of the article within quotation marks
3. Name of the book, journal, or complete work, italicized
4. Publication information
   Place, publisher, and date for books

Volume and year of a journal
Exact date of a magazine
Date and description for government documents
5. URL (Uniform Resource Locator), within angle brackets
6. Date of your access, followed by a period

NOTE: Do not include page numbers unless the Internet article shows original page numbers from the printed version of the journal or magazine. Do not include the total number of paragraphs nor specific paragraph numbers.

World Wide Web sites

Online Journal

Banning, E. B. "Herders or Homesteaders? A
Neolithic Farm in Wadi Ziqlab, Jordan."
Biblical Archaeologist 58.1 (March 1995).
<http://scholar.cc.emory.edu/scripts/ASOR/
BA/Banning.html> 9 April 1997.

Abstract of a Journal Article

Kassim, Saul M. "The Psychology of Confession
Evidence." *American Psychologist* 52 (1997).
Abstract.
<http://www.apa.org/journals/amp397
tc.html> 10 Apr. 1997.

Online Magazine

Cohoon, Sharon, Jim McCausland, and Lauren Bonar
Swezey. "Secrets of the Garden Masters:
Heims's Secrets." *Sunset* Sept. 1996.
<http://pathfinder.com@AiRYiAYAC5LGsKR/

```
...Sunset/1996/September/features/heims.htm
   l> 4 Mar. 1997.
```

Fahey, Todd Brendan. "Beach House." *Kudzu* Autumn
    1995.
    <http://www.etext.org/Zines/K954/ Fahey-
    Beach.html> 10 Mar. 1997.

Online Magazine, No Author listed

"Health-Care Inflation: It's Baaack!" *Business
    Week* 17 Mar. 1997.
    <http://www.businessweek.com/1997/11/
    b351852.htm> 18 March 1997.

Government Document

United States. Cong. Senate. *Superfund Cleanup
    Acceleration Act of 1997.* 21 Jan. 1997.
    105th Cong. Senate Bill 8.
    <http.thomas.loc. gov/egi-bin/query/
    2?C105:S.8:> 4 March 1997.

Gopher Sites

D'Agour, Armand. Review of *Classical Women
    Poets*, by Josephine Balmer, ed. and trans.
    Newcastle-upon-Tyne: Bloodaxe Books, 1996.
    <gopher://gopher.lib.virginia.edu:70/alpha
    /bmer/v97/97-I-4> 10 Mar. 1997.
Diamond, Richard. "Seeing One's Way: The Image
    and   Action of "Oidipous Tyrannos."

Electronic Antiquity 1 (1993).
<gopher://gopher.info. edu.au> 6 March
1997.

"No One Scientific Study Can Tell All."
<gopher://gopher.fhcrc.org:70/0waisdocid%3.
..mer_Quest_ 1994/SciNews> 10 March 1997.

Listserv (Email Discussion Group)

Camilleri, Rosemary. "Narrative Bibliography."
10 Mar. 1997.
Listserv <H-RHETOR @msu.edu> 11 Mar. 1997.

Selber, Stuart A. "CFP:CPTSC" [Call for Position
Papers: Council for Programs in Technical
and Scientific Communication] 7 Mar. 1997.
Listserv <H-RHETOR@msu.edu> 11 Mar. 1997.

Linkage data (a file accessed from another file)

"What Happens to Recycled Plastics?" Lkd. Better
World Discussion Topics at Recycling
Discussion Group. 1996.
<http://www. betterworld.com/BWZ/
9602/learn.htm> 18 June 1997.

Newsgroups

Anders, Jelmert. "Global Warming/Climate Change:

A New Approach." 21 Feb. 1997.
Newsgroup <sci.environment> 11 Mar. 1997.

Link, Richard. "Territorial Fish." 11 Jan. 1997.
Newsgroup <rec.aquaria.freshwater. misc> 11
Mar. 1997.

HyperNews

Ochberg, Abigail. "Algae-based Paper." Recycling
Discussion Group, 9 Oct. 1996.
HyperNews posting <http://www.
betterworld.com/BWDiscuss/get/recycleD.
html?embed=2> 18 June 1997.

Telnet Site

U. S. Navel Observatory. "The Mercury Ion
Frequency Standard."
Telnet <duke.ldgo. columbia.edu/port=23
login ads, set terminal to 8/N/1> 6 Mar.
1997.

FTP Site

Kranidiotis, Argiris A. "Human Audio Perception
Frequently Asked Questions." 7 June 1994.
<ftp://svr-ftp.eng.cam.ac.uk/ pub/comp.
speech/info/HumanAudioPerception> 11 March
1997.

CD-ROM

Material cited from a CD-ROM requires different forms. If you are citing from an abstract on CD-ROM (InfoTrac, Silverplatter, UMI-Proquest), use this form:

Figueredo, Aurelio J., and Laura Ann McCloskey.
     "Sex, Money, and Paternity: The
     Evolutionary Psychology of Domestic
     Violence." *Ethnology and Sociobiology* 14
     (1993): 353-79. Abstract. *PsychLIT*. CD-ROM.
     SilverPlatter. 1993.

For a full-text article found on CD-ROM, use the following form:

Wessel, David. "Fed Lifts Rates Half Point,
     Setting Four-Year High." *Wall Street
     Journal*. 2 Feb. 1995: A2+. *Wall Street
     Journal Ondisc*. CD-ROM. UMI-ProQuest. 1995.

For an encyclopedia article on CD-ROM, use the following form:

"Abolitionist Movement." *Compton's Interactive
     Encyclopedia*. CD-ROM. Softkey Multimedia.
     1996.

4

Citing Electronic Sources in APA STYLE

The American Psychological Association has established a Web site that, among other things, explains its method for citing Internet sources. Consult this URL:

> http://www.apa.org/journals/webref.html

At this site, Leslie Cameron, Director of APA Journals, provides instructions that supercede those in the 1994 *Publication Manual of the American Psychological Association,* 4th edition. Also available from APA is a site that answers frequently asked questions about APA style. Consult this URL:

> http://www.apa.org/journals/faq.html

APA Style for In-Text Citations

As in MLA style above, material from electronic sources presents special problems when you are writing in APA style. Currently, most Internet sources have no prescribed page numbers or numbered paragraphs. You cannot list a screen number because monitors differ. You cannot list the page numbers of a downloaded document because computer printers differ. Therefore, in most cases, do not list a page number or a paragraph number. Here are basic rules.

1. **Omit a page or paragraph number.** The marvelous feature of electronic text is that its searchable, so your readers can find your quotation quickly with the FIND feature. Suppose that you have written the following:

> The UCLA Television Violence Report (1996)
> advises against making the television industry
> the "scapegoat for violence" by advocating a

> focus on "deadlier and more significant causes:
> inadequeate parenting, drugs, underclass rage,
> unemployment and availability of weaponry."

A reader who wants to investigate further will find your complete citation on your Works Cited page. There the reader will discover the Internet address for the article. After finding the article via a browser, (e.g., Netscape or Internet Explorer), the investigator can press EDIT, then FIND, and then type in a key phrase, such as *scapegoat for violence*. The software will immediately move the cursor to the passage shown above. That's much easier than counting through 46 paragraphs.

2. **Provide a paragraph number**. Some academic societies are urging scholars who write on the Internet to number their paragraphs. So if you find an article on the Internet that has numbered paragraphs, by all means supply that information in your citation.

> The Insurance Institute for Highway Safety
> (1997) emphasizes restraint first, saying,
> "Riding unrestrained or improperly restrained in
> a motor vehicle always has been the greatest
> hazard for children" (par. 13).

> The most common type of diabetes is non-insulin-
> dependent-diabetes mellitus (NIDDM), which
> "affects 90% of those with diabetes and usually
> appears after age 40" (Larson, 1996, par. 3).

3. **Provide a page number**. In a few instances, you will find page numbers buried within brackets here and there throughout an article. These refer to the page numbers of the printed version of the document. In these cases, you should cite the page just as you would a printed source. Note this example:

> De-nationalizing does not mean abolishing difference but abolishing the myth of identity that regulated and policed difference upholds. Thus, what is required is a reading of the frontiers and borders that are at /pp 17-18/ work within and against the pretensions to "greatness," to majority, of any national literature. That is to say, a finding of the minor and the evocation of its difference where it is not expected.

Readings (1991) has argued that each literary culture should identify the minor literature as a part of its national identity, not just elevate its majority literature as its "greatness" (pp. 17-18).

World Wide Web Site

Dove (1997) has made the distinction between a Congressional calendar day and a legislative day, noting, "A legislative day is the period of time following an adjournment of the Senate until another adjournment."

"Psychologically oriented techniques used to elicit confessions may undermine their validity" (Kassin, 1997, abstract).

Commenting on Neolithic sites of the Southern Levant in *Biblical Archaeologist*, Banning (1995) has argued the "Natufians set the stage for the development of large villages with an increasing reliance on cereal grains and legumes that could be cultivated." Banning's work has shown that small villages often existed for a time only to disappear mysteriously, perhaps because of plagues, invaders, or--most likely--a nomadic way of life.

Citing Cyberspace

Email

The Publication Manual of the American Psychological Association stipulates that personal communications, which others cannot retrieve, should be cited in the text only and not mentioned at all in the bibliography. However, electronic chat groups have gained legitimacy in recent years, so in the text give an exact date and provide the Email address *only* if the citation has scholarly relevance and *only* if the author has made public the Email address with the expressed wish for correspondence.

One technical writing instructor (March 8, 1997) has bemoaned the inability of hardware developers to maintain pace with the ingenuity of software developers. In his Email message, he indicated that educational institutions cannot keep pace with the hardware developers. Thus, "students nationwide suffer with antiquated equipment, even though it's only a few years old"(ClemmerJ@ APSU01.APSU.EDU).

If the Email is part of a network or online journal, it *should be* listed in the bibliography. In such cases, use the form shown next under "Listserv" and see the bibliography form on page 42.

Listserv (Email Discussion Group)

Camilleri (May 7, 1997) has identified the book *Storyteller* for those interested in narrative bibliography.

Funder (April 5, 1997) has argued against the "judgmental process."

Citing Cyberspace

HyperNews Posting

Ochberg (1996) has commented on the use of algae in paper that "initially has a green tint to it, but unlike bleached paper, which turns yellow with age, this algae paper becomes whiter with age."

Gopher Site

In an essay in *Electronic Antiquity*, Diamond (1993) has explored the issue of psychological blindness in *Oedipus Rex*:

> Thus Sophokles has us ask the question, who is blind? We must answer that Teiresias is physically blind, yet he sees himself and Oidipous' nature. Oidipous is physically sighted, but he is blind to himself, to his own nature.

NOTE: For long indented quotations, the paragraph reference goes *outside* the cited material, as shown immediately above.

Online Magazine

In *Kudzu*, Fahey (1995) described one of his characters in "Beach House" as a psychological wreck:

> Johnny was, by my estimation, a Casualty, though a functional one. He walked

everywhere, and everywhere he walked, a
bright, pleasant grin stretched his facial
muscles, and he looked like a carpenter who
had plied his trade well.

BusinessWeek (1997) reported that health-care
inflation seems determined to climb because
medical costs are increasing and could "hit
double digits."

Government Document

The Web site *Thomas* (1997) has provided the
four-page outline to the *Superfund Cleanup
Acceleration Act of 1997*, which will provoke
community participation, enforce remedial
actions, establish liability, and protect
natural resources.

FTP Sites

Kranidiotis (1994) has shown in the following
graph that perceptually "all the sounds
corresponding to the points on the curve have
the same intensity: this means that the ear has
a large range where it is nearly linear (1000 to
8000 Hz), achieving better results on a little
domain."

CD-ROM

Compton's Interactive Encyclopedia (1996) has explained that the Abolition Society, which originated in England in 1787, appears to be the first organized group in opposition to slavery. Later, in 1823, the Anti-Slavery Society was formed by Thomas Fowell Buxton, who wielded power as a member of Parliament.

APA Bibliography Entries

The following information conforms to the instructions of APA. When citing sources in the "References" of your APA-style paper, provide this information if available:

1. Author/editor last name, followed by a comma and the initials
2. Year of publication, followed by a comma, then month and day for magazines and newspapers, within parentheses
3. Title of the article, not within quotations and with only major words capitalized, followed by the total number of paragraphs within brackets only if that information is provided (for an example, see the Trehin citation on the next page). Note: You need not count the paragraphs yourself; in fact, it's better that you don't.
4. Name of the book, journal, or complete work, italicized, if one is listed
5. Volume number, if listed, italicized
6. Page numbers only if you have that data from a printed version of the journal or magazine. If the periodical has no volume number, use "p." or "pp." before the numbers; if the journal has a volume number, omit "p." or "pp.")
7. The word "Retrieved," followed by the date of access, followed by the source (e.g. World Wide Web or Telnet) and a colon
8. The URL (URLs can be quite long, but you will need to provide the full data for other researchers to find the source.)

Citing Cyberspace

Note: The APA style manual is very clear about the margins for bibliography entries. If you are preparing a draft to go to a journal for publication, you should use a paragraph indention and underlining, as shown:

Banning, E. B. (1995). Herders or homesteaders? A neolithic farm in Wadi Ziqlab, Jordan. <u>Biblical Archaeologist, 58.</u> Retrieved March 9, 1997 from the World Wide Web: http://scholar.cc.emory.edu/scripts /ASOR/BA/ Banning.html

However, if your research paper is being printed as a final document for your instructor, or if your research paper will be published on a Web site, you should use the hanging indention of three (3) spaces and, if available, use the italics font for titles and volume numbers, as shown in the next few examples. That is, you are "publishing" the paper for the instructor or—of more importance—you are publishing the paper on a Web site. Remember this: national journals will reset a draft copy into hanging indentions for publication; however, as a student you must "publish" your own paper.

World Wide Web Sites

Online Journal

Trehin, P. (1994). Computer aided teaching. [6 paragraphs]. Computer Technology and Autism, 15. Retrieved April 28, 1997 from the World Wide Web:http://web.syr.edu/~jmwobus/autism/ INK.htm#Section_1.0.1

Abstract from an Online Journal

Kassim, S. M. (1997). The psychology of

confession evidence. [Abstract]. *American Psychologist, 52.* Retrieved April 10, 1997 from the World Wide Web: http://www.apa.org/ journals/amp397tc.html

Online Magazine

Cohoon, S., McCausland, J., & Swezey, L. B. (1996, September). Secrets of the garden masters: Heims's secrets. *Sunset.* Retrieved March 4, 1997 from the World Wide Web: http/pathfinder.com@AiRYiAYAC5LGs KR/ ...Sunset/1996/ September/features/ heims.html

Fahey, T. B. (1995, Autumn). *Beach house. Kudzu, 3.* Retrieved March 10, 1997 from the World Wide Web: http://www.etext.org/Zines/K954/ Fahey-Beach.html

Online Magazine, No Author listed

Health-care inflation: It's baaack! (1997, March 17). *Business Week, 56-62.* Retrieved March 18, 1997 from the World Wide Wide: http://www.businessweek.com/1997/11/ b351852.html

Bulletins and Government Documents

Edelson, S. B. (1995). Autism: An environmental maladaptation. Environment and Preventive

Health Center of America. Retrieved from the
World Wide Web: http://www.
envprevhealthctratl.com/env-mal.htm

U.S. Cong. Senate. (1997, January 21). *Superfund
cleanup acceleration act of 1997*. Senate
Bill 8. Retrieved from the World Wide Web:
http.thomas.loc.gov/egi-bin/query/
2?C105:S.8:

Hypernews Posting

Ochberg, A. (Oct. 9, 1996). Algae-based paper.
Recycling Discussion Group. Retrieved June
18, 1997, from the World Wide Web:
http://www. betterworld.com/ BWDiscuss/
get/recycleD. html?embed=2

Gopher Site

D'Agour, A. (1996). Classical women poets [4
paragraphs]. [Review of the book *Classical
women poets*]. Retrieved March 10, 1997 from
gopher://gopher.lib.virginia.edu:70/alpha/
bmer/v97/97-I-4

Diamond, R. (1993). Seeing one's way: The image
and action of *Oidipous Tyrannos* [13
paragraphs]. *Electronic Antiquity, 1.*

Retrieved March 6, 1997 from gopher:
gopher//gopher.info.edu.au

No one scientific study can tell all. (1997,
March 10). Retrieved March 10, 1997 from
gopher:gopher.fhcrc.org:70/
0waisdocid%3...mer_Quest_1994/SciNews

Linkage data (a file accessed from another file)

What happens to recycled plastics? (1996). Lkd.
Better world discussion topics at Recycling
discussion group. Retrieved June 18, 1997
from http://www.betterworld.com/BWZ/9602/
learn.htm

Listserv (Email Discussion Group)

Camilleri, R. (1997, March 10). Narrative
bibliography. Retrieved March 11, 1997 from
Email: H-RHETOR@msu.edu

Newsgroups

Anders, J. (1997, February 21). Global
warming/climate change: A new approach.
Institute of Marine Research. Retrieved
March 11, 1997 from Usenet: cgi-bin/news?msg
@44430/sci.environment/330DE368.4CC8@imr.no

Link, R. (1997, January 11). Territorial fish.
    Southwest Research Institute. Retrieved
    March 10, 1997 from Usenet: cgi-
    bin...@10016/rec.aquaria. freshwater.misc/
    5b9u9p$kod@pemrac.space.swri.edu

Telnet Site

U. S. Naval Observatory. The mercury ion
    frequency standard. Retrieved March 6, 1997
    from Telnet 192.5,41.239/duke.ldgo.
    columbia.edu /port=23 login ads, set
    terminal to 8/N/1

FTP Site

Kranidiotis, A. A. (1994, June 7). Human audio
    perception frequently asked questions.
    Retrieved March 11, 1997 from FTP: svr-
    ftp.eng.cam.ac.uk/pub/comp.speech/info/
    HumanAudioPerception

CD-ROM

Material cited from a CD-ROM requires different forms. If you are
citing from an abstract on CD-ROM, use this form:

Figueredo, A. J., & McCloskey, L.A. (1993).
    Sex,money, and paternity: The evolutionary
    psychology of domestic violence [CD-ROM].

Ethnology and Sociobiology, 14, 353-79.
Abstract from SilverPlatter File: *PsychLIT*
item: 81-3654

For an encyclopedia article on CD-ROM, use this form:

Abolitionist movement [CD-ROM]. (1996).
Compton's interactive encyclopedia. New York:
Softkey Multimedia.

For a full-text article found on CD-ROM, use the following form:

Wessel, D. (1995, February 2). Fed lifts rates
    half point, setting four-year high [CD-ROM].
    Wall Street Journal, p. A2+. Article from
    UMI-ProQuest file: *Wall Street Journal
    Ondisc* Item 34561

5

Citing Electronic Sources in the Chicago Footnote System

The fine arts and some fields in the humanities (not literature) employ traditional footnotes, which should conform to standards set by the *The Chicago Manual of Style*, 14th ed., 1993. With this system, you must employ superscript numerals within the text and place a footnote at the bottom of the page (although some instructors allow *endnotes;* that is, all your notes are gathered on one page at the end of your paper).

Using Superscript Numerals in Your Text

In your text use Arabic numerals typed slightly above the line (like this[15]) to signal a citation that will be found in a footnote or endnote. Place this superscript numeral at the end of quotations or paraphrases, with the numeral following immediately without a space after the final word or mark of punctuation, as in these examples:

Robert B. Dove makes the distinction between a Congressional calendar day and a legislative day, noting, "A legislative day is the period of time following an adjournment of the Senate until another adjournment."[1]

Commenting on Neolithic sites of the Southern Levant in the online magazine *Biblical Archaeologist*, E. B. Banning argues the "Natufians set the stage for the development of large villages with an increasing reliance on cereal grains and legumes that could be cultivated."[2] Banning's work shows that small villages often existed for a time only to disappear mysteriously, perhaps because of plagues, invaders, or--most likely--a nomadic way of life.[3]

In an essay in *Electronic Antiquity*, Richard Diamond explores the issue of blindness in *Oedipus Rex*:

> Thus Sophokles has us ask the question, who is blind? We must answer that Teiresias is physically blind, yet he sees himself and Oidipous' nature. Oidipous is physically sighted, but he is blind to himself, to his own nature.[4]

Abigail Ochberg has commented on the use of algae in paper that "initially has a green tint to it, but unlike bleached paper which turns yellow with age, this algae paper becomes whiter with age."[5]

Writing the Footnotes

Place your footnotes at the bottom of pages to correspond with superscript numerals. Some papers require footnotes on almost every page. Follow these conventions:

1. Use single spacing within each footnote, but use a double-space

between footnotes.

2. Indent the first line five spaces.
3. Number the footnotes consecutively throughout the entire paper.
4. Collect at the bottom of each page all the footnotes to citations made on this page (or gather all notes at the end of your paper).
5. Distinguish footnotes from the text by (1) using a smaller type size, (2) triple-spacing, or (3) placing a 12-space bar line beginning at the left margin.
6. Cite electronic sources in this general order:

> author
> title of article
> the text in which the article appears, preceded by *in*
> the type of online source, within brackets [database online]
> publication data within parentheses; that is, the place, publisher, volume, and date, as appropriate, with the date that *you* cited the source within brackets *inside* the parentheses, followed by a semicolon
> the address, preceded by *available from*

Online Journal

1. E. B. Banning, "Herders or Homesteaders? A Neolithic Farm in Wadi Ziqlab, Jordan," in Biblical Archaeologist [online journal] (vol. 58.1, March 1995 [cited 9 April 1997]); available from World Wide Web @ http://scholar.cc.emory.edu/scripts/ ASOR/BA/Banning.html

Online Magazine

2. Jon Guttman, "Constitution: The Legendary Survivor," in *Military History* [online magazine] (1997 [cited 28 April 1997]); available from World Wide Web @

http://www.thehistorynet.com/M...ry/articles/
1997/0297-text.htm

Online Magazine, No Author listed

3. "Health-Care Inflation: It's Baaack!"
in *Business Week* [magazine online] (17 Mar. 1997
[cited 18 March 1997]); available from World
Wide Web @ http://www.businessweek.com/1997/
11/b351852.htm

Government Document

4. United States Congress, Senate,
Superfund Cleanup Acceleration Act of 1997
[database online] (105th Cong., Senate Bill 8,
21 January 1997 [cited 4 March   1997]);
available from World Wide Web @
http.thomas.loc.gov/egi-bin/query/ 2?C105:S.8:

Gopher Site

5. Richard Diamond, "Seeing One's Way: The
Image and Action of "Oidipous Tyrannos," in
Electronic Antiquity [magazine online] (vol. 1,
1993 [cited 6 March 1997]); available from
gopher @ gopher.info.edu.au

6. Armand D'Agour, review of *Classical
Women Poets*, by Josephine Balmer, ed. and trans.

[electronic bulletin board] (Newcastle-upon-
Tyne: Bloodaxe Books, 1996 [cited 10 March
1997]); available from gopher @
gopher.lib.virginia.edu: 70/alpha/bmer/v97/
97-I-4

Listserv (Email Discussion Group)

7. Rosemary Camilleri, "Narrative
Bibliography" [electronic bulletin board](10
March 1997 [cited 11 March 1997]); available
from listserv @ H-RHETOR @msu.edu

Newsgroups

8. Richard Link, "Territorial Fish,"
[electronic newsgroup] (11 Jan. 1997 [cited 14
March 1997]); available from listserv@
rec.aquaria.freshwater.misc

Telnet Site

9. United States Navel Observatory, "The
Mercury Ion Frequency Standard" [electronic
bulletin board] (cited 6 March 1997); available
from Telnet @ duke.ldgo.columbia.edu/port=23
login ads, set terminal to 8/N/1

FTP Site

10. Argiris A. Kranidiotis, "Human Audio
Perception Frequently Asked Questions"
[electronic bulletin board] (7 June 1994 [cited
11 March 1997]); available from ftp://svr-
ftp.eng.cam.ac.uk/pub/comp.
speech/info/HumanAudio Perception

HyperNews

11. Abigail Ochberg, "Algae-based Paper."
[Recycling Discussion Group] (9 Oct. 1996 [cited
18 June 1997]); available from HyperNews posting
http://www.betterworld.com/BWDiscuss/get/
recycleD.html?embed=2

Linkage Data (a file accessed from another file)

12. "What Happens to Recycled Plastics?"
[Lkd. Better World Discussion Topics at
Recycling Discussion Group] (1996 [cited 18 June
1997]); available from World Wide Web @
http://www. betterworld.com/BWZ/ 9602/learn.htm

CD-ROM

13. "Abolitionist Movement," in *Compton's
Interactive Encyclopedia* [CD-ROM] (Softkey
Multimedia, 1996 [cited 11 March 1996]).

14. David Wessel, "Fed Lifts Rates Half
Point, Setting Four-Year High," in *Wall Street
Journal* [CD-ROM] (*Wall Street Journal Ondisc* 2
February 1995: A2+ [cited 6 February 1996]);
available from UMI-ProQuest.

15. Aureliio J. Figueredo and Laura Ann
McCloskey, "Sex, Money, and Paternity: The
Evolutionary Psychology of Domestic Violence,"
in *Ethnology and Sociobiology,* abstract (vol.
14, 1993: 353-79 [cited 12 March 1997]);
available from *PsychLIT* SilverPlatter.

Subsequent References to a Source

After a first full reference, shorten future footnotes to the source by giving
only the name of the author (or title). If an author has two works
mentioned, employ a shortened version of the title with the author's name
(e.g., 3. Smith, "Cloning").

14. Diamond.
15. Fahey, "Beach House."
16. Fahey, "End Run."

The Latin abbreviations *op. cit* and *loc. cit.* are no longer used, but *The
Chicago Manual of Style* does permit the use of *ibid.* to refer to the
source cited in the previous note.

17. Diamond.
18. Ibid.

Bibliography

In addition to footnotes or endnotes, you may need to supply a separate bibliography that lists all sources in alphabetical order. Use hanging indention for the entries; that is, keyboard the first line of each entry flush left but indent the second line and other succeeding lines five spaces. Alphabetize the list by last names of authors. List alphabetically by title two or more works by one author.

The bibliography will give the same basic information as the footnote except for three differences. First, use periods, not commas, to separate elements. Second, do not number the entries. Third, do not provide a reference to a specific paragraph. If available, do list the total number of paragraphs or online pages (with the understanding, of course, that these pages may reproduce differently on various computer printers). The basic examples are shown here.

Banning, E. B. "Herders or Homesteaders? A
    Neolithic Farm in Wadi Ziqlab, Jordan." In
    Biblical Archaeologist [online journal].
    Vol. 58.1, March 1995 [cited 9 April
    1997]. Available from World Wide Web @
    http://scholar.cc.emory.edu/scripts/
    ASOR/BA/Banning.html [9 pages.]

Fahey, Todd Brendan. "Beach House." In *Kudzu*
    [online magazine]. Autumn 1995 [cited 10
    March 1997]. Available from World Wide
    Web @ http://www.etext.org/Zines/
    K954/Fahey-Beach.html [42 paragraphs.]

"Health-Care Inflation: It's Baaack!" In
    Business Week [magazine online]. 17 Mar.
    1997 [cited 18 March 1997]. Available from

World Wide Web @
http://www.businessweek.com/1997/
11/b351852.htm [8 paragraphs.]

United States Congress. Senate. *Superfund
Cleanup Acceleration Act of 1997*
[database online]. 105th Cong., Senate
Bill 8, 21 January 1997 [cited 4 March
1997]. Available from World Wide Web @
http.thomas. loc.gov/egi-bin/query/
2?C105:S.8: [12 pages]

6

Citing Electronic Sources in the CBE Documentation Style

A number system for documentation is used by writers in the applied sciences (chemistry, computer science, engineering, mathematics, and physics) and the medical sciences (bio-medicine, health, medicine, and nursing). In simple terms, it requires an in-text *number*, often to the exclusion of the author's name. The references at the end of the paper correspond to this number.

This style is set by *The CBE Style Manual for Authors, Editors, and Publishers*, 6th edition, 1994. The initialization stands for Council of Biology Editors. In truth, the CBE guide advocates two styles, one very similar to the APA style that uses an author's name and the year in parenthetical citations and one that uses the numbers. The number style is discussed here. If your instructor prefers the author/year system, refer to pages 00-00.

Assigning the numbers

Use one of two plans. Most writers use plan 1.

Plan 1: As you write your paper, you may assign numbers, consecutively, based on the order in which you cite your sources. The first will be 1, the second 2, and so forth. With this system, your list of references at the end of the paper will *not* be in alphabetical order.

Plan 2: Gather all of your references in alphabetical order and number them consecutively (in which case, of course, the numbers will not appear in consecutive order in the text).

Selecting a Numbering Method

You may use raised superscript numerals[5] or numbers within parentheses (5) or numbers within brackets [5]. Consult with your instructor about the method preferred.

In-text Citations

Many writers use numbers alone without the name of the author or page number, although these may be included. Note these examples:

It is known (1) that the DNA concentration of a nucleus doubles during interphase.

In particular, the recent paper by Hershel, Hobbs, and Thomason (2) has raised many interesting questions related to photosynthesis, some of which were answered by Skelton (3,4).

The results of the respiration experiment published by Jones (5, Table 6, par. 12) had been predicted earlier by Smith (6, Proposition 8).

It has been noted (6) that the use of algae in paper that "initially has a green tint to it" will produce a paper that "becomes whiter with age" (par. 1).

If you refer to a source that you have previously cited, use the original number again. That is, each source has only one number.

Numbering the List of References

Label your bibliography page "References." Number each entry with an Arabic numeral. Place them in alphabetical order or in the order of your citations (see "Selecting a Numbering Method." Use this order:

Author
Title of article or chapter
Name of journal or book
Description within brackets, such as "[journal online]"
Publication date, followed by a semicolon
Number of paragraphs, followed by a period
The electronic address preceded by "Available from:"
The word "Accessed," followed by the date that you accessed the material

Conform to these examples:

1. Trehin, P. Computer aided teaching. Computer Technology and Autism [serial online] 1994, No. 15; 6 par. Available from: http://web. syr.edu/-jmwobus /autism/LINK.htm# Section_1.0.1 Accessed 1997 Apr. 26.

2. Edelson, SB. Autism: An environmental maladaptation [bulletin online] 1995; 3 pars. Available from: http://www. envprevhealthctratl.comj/env_mal.htm Accessed 1997 Apr. 26.

3. Boyle, TD. Diagnosing autism and other pervasive developmental disorders [article online] no date; 19 par. Available from: http://www.injersey.com/Living/ Health/ Autism/page3.html Accessed 1997 Apr. 26.

4. Hohmann, K. Autism as a motor disorder bulletin online] 1997 Apr. 14; 1 par. Available from: listserv innugapl-int.news.prodigy.com Accessed 1997 Apr. 26.

5. Autism and brain development research laboratory [bulletin online] 1997 Feb. 25; 3 par. Available from: http://nodulus.extern. ucsd.edu/ Accessed 1997 Apr. 26.
6. Algae-based paper [HyperNews posting]1996 Oct. 9; 1 par. Available from:http://www. betterworld.com/BWDiscuss/get/recycled. html?embed=2